Y0-CLI-202

Ceil and David Olivestone

LET'S GO TO SYNAGOGUE

Illustrated by Arieh Zeldich

SBS PUBLISHING, INC.

For Naftali

Text copyright © 1981 by Ceil and David Olivestone.

Illustrations copyright © 1981 by Arieh Zeldich.

All rights reserved. No part of this publication may be
reproduced, stored in a retrieval system, or transmitted,
in any form or by any means, electronic, mechanical,
photocopying, recording, or otherwise, without permission
in writing from the Publisher.

SBS Publishing, Inc.
14 West Forest Avenue
Englewood, N.J. 07631

Library of Congress Cataloging in Publication Data

Olivestone, Ceil, 1950—
   Let's go to synagogue.

   Summary; Depicts the highlights of the synagogue
service.
   1.   Sabbath—Juvenile literature.   2.   Synagogues—
Juvenile literature. [1. Sabbath. 2. Synagogues]
I. Olivestone, David, 1944—   II. Zeldich,
Arieh, 1949—   III. Title.
BM685.037   296.4'1   81-516
ISBN 0-89961-018-8   AACR2

Printed in Israel by Peli Printing Works Ltd.
9 8 7 6 5 4 3 2 1

It's Shabbat.

Let's go to synagogue.

Here it is.

Come inside

and find a place to sit.

Now take a siddur.

It's in Hebrew.

Don't open it like an English book—

it starts from the other end.

There's a man unfolding his tallit.

He puts it around him.

Watch how it swings when he moves.

The chazan begins to sing.

His voice is so lovely,

he makes us want to sing along with him.

It's time to open the ark

and take the Torah out.

The chazan holds it

and sings Shema Yisrael.

Then he slowly marches around with it.

Get ready to kiss the Torah!

You know it's coming

when you hear the bells tinkling.

Listen to the reading of the Torah.

When it's finished

a man lifts it up for us all to see.

It looks very heavy—

but he mustn't drop it.

Next the Rabbi speaks.

He is very smart.

Everybody sits and listens to him.

Sitting still can sometimes be difficult.

Now stand up

and quietly read the siddur.

Soon the chazan starts to sing again.

Singing out loud is the best of all!

It's almost time to go home.

But first everybody sings

Alenu and Adon Olam.

Before you leave,

say Shabbat Shalom to all your friends.

See you again next week.

Shabbat Shalom!

NOTES FOR PARENTS

SYNAGOGUE: we chose the most common word but you may wish to substitute shul, or temple, according to your preference.

SIDDUR: prayer book.

TALLIT: prayer shawl.

CHAZAN: cantor who leads the service.

TORAH: scroll of the Five Books of Moses.

ARK: where the Torah scrolls are kept.

SHEMA YISRAEL: "Hear, O Israel", from Deuteronomy 6:4.

ALENU: concluding prayer.

ADON OLAM: concluding hymn.

SHABBAT SHALOM: Sabbath greeting.